MAPS & MAPMAKERS

MAPS & MAPMAKERS

Mapping Our World

Martyn Bramwell

Illustrated by George Fryer

Lerner Publications Company • Minneapolis

This edition published in 1998

Lerner Publications Company
241 First Avenue North
Minneapolis MN 55401

© Graham Beehag Books

Printed in Italy by Vallardi Industrie Grafich s.p.a.
Bound in the United States of America

Library of Congress Cataloging-in-Publication Data

Bramwell, Martyn.
    Mapping our world / by Martyn Bramwell.
        p.   cm. – (Maps & mapmakers)
    Includes index.
    Summary: Uses various kinds of maps along with text to describe many aspects of this earth including its history and changing conditions.
    ISBN 0-8225-2924-8 (lib. bdg. : alk. paper)
    1. Cartography–Juvenile literature.   [1. Cartography. 2.Maps.]
I. Title. II. Series: Bramwell, Martyn. Maps & mapmakers.
GA130.B645   1998
528–DC21   97-50150

Acknowledgments

Thanks to Panos Pictures for use of the picture on page 27, and the bottom picture on page 30, Corbis UK for the top picture on page 30, and the Canadian Tourist Board for the picture on page 33,

Contents

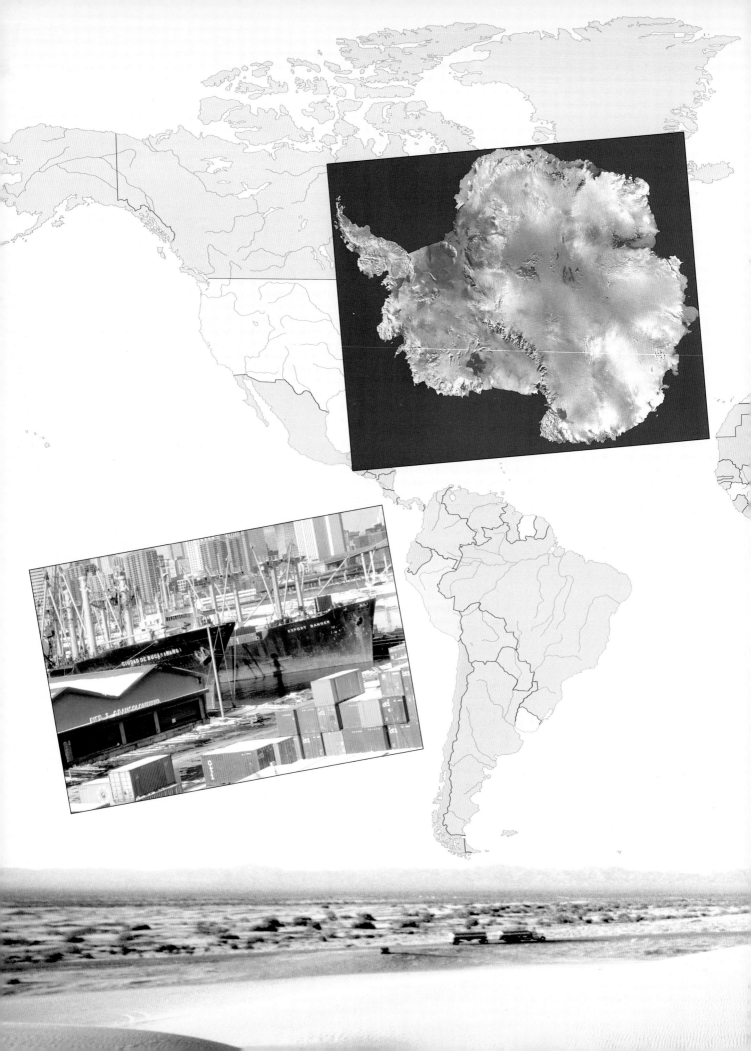

Introduction

Two hundred years ago, the fastest way to travel overland was by horse. The only way a person in the United States could communicate with someone in Europe was by letter, which could take months to arrive. And farmers planted and harvested their crops using horse-drawn plows and hand tools. Seafarers had charted most of the world's coastlines, but mapmakers (cartographers) hadn't mapped the continents' interiors, and Antarctica hadn't yet been visited.

The world has changed a lot since then. In the nineteenth century, steam engines provided power for farm tractors and harvesters and for factories making everything from clothes and shoes to nails and rifles. Steamships carried passengers and trade goods across the oceans, and railroads crisscrossed the land. Over the years, explorers filled in more and more of the world map–North and South America, Africa, Australia, and Antarctica. Early in the twentieth century, steam gave way to the gas-powered engine, and in less than 100 years, transport technology graduated from the Model T Ford and the Wright brothers' *Kitty Hawk* to air-conditioned cars and 600-seat airplanes. New technologies appeared at a breathtaking pace. We can watch television programs from all over the world and communicate with telephones and computers. Our homes are full of plastics, nylon, and other synthetic materials. And many of the world's once-fatal diseases can be cured.

These changes have even had an impact on mapping. We can map ocean currents, crop distribution, pollution, and the path of forest fires with cameras orbiting miles above the earth. Informational maps that show differences in the distribution of the world's **resources** can help us study economic imbalances. Maps lead us to a better understanding of the world we live in.

Continents and Oceans

Mount Everest's summit in Asia's Himalaya Mountains is almost 5.5 miles above sea level. The deepest part of the Marianas Trench in the western Pacific Ocean is 6.8 miles below sea level. That's a difference of more than 12 miles, yet in proportion to the size of the earth it barely shows. The earth's rocky outer surface, which geologists call the **crust**, really has no more highs and lows than the skin of an orange.

Land covers about 29 percent of the earth's surface–a total area of more than 57 million square miles. Divided into seven large areas called **continents**, this land surface, or **topography**, varies from rugged mountain ranges to smooth, flat plains depending on the continent's geological history. But whether the land is covered by **tropical rain forest**, grassland, desert, or **tundra** depends on where the continent lies on the earth's surface, its altitude (distance above sea level), and in which direction the rain-bearing winds blow.

The other 71 percent of the earth's surface is water–the seas, oceans, and moisture-laden atmosphere that give the earth its brilliant blue color when seen from space. Not long ago, no one knew what lay deep within the oceans, but since the 1960s, marine scientists have discovered an amazing underwater landscape with vast mountain ranges, submarine volcanoes, and unusual forms of life. These discoveries have unlocked the secrets of our planet's ancient history and have explained why the continents and oceans are the shape they are and how the mountain ranges formed.

The Earth's Highs and Lows
The map above shows the main geographical features of the earth's surface–the mountain ranges, rivers, deserts, and plains. These huge features can be seen clearly from satellites orbiting high above.

The Deepest Ocean Trenches

Ocean	Trench	Depth
Atlantic	Puerto Rico Trench	28,374 feet
	South Sandwich Trench	27,108 feet
Indian	Romanche Trench	25,356 feet
	Weber Deep	25,344 feet
	Sunda Trench	24,452 feet
South Pacific	Tonga Trench	35,435 feet
	Kermadec Trench	32,964 feet
West Pacific	Marianas Trench	36,198 feet
	Philippine Trench	32,908 feet
East Pacific	Aleutian Trench	26,574 feet
	Peru-Chile Trench	26,412 feet

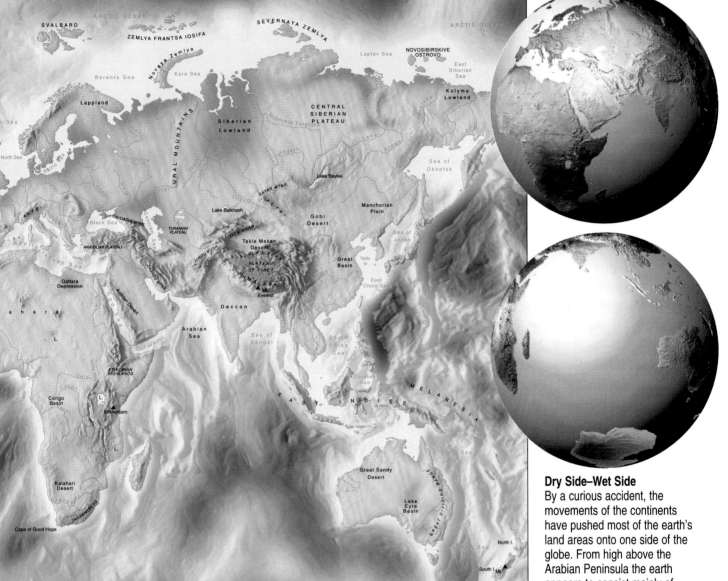

Dry Side–Wet Side
By a curious accident, the movements of the continents have pushed most of the earth's land areas onto one side of the globe. From high above the Arabian Peninsula the earth appears to consist mainly of land, but from high above the Pacific Ocean it appears to be 90 percent water.

The Highest Peaks

Africa	Kilimanjaro (Tanzania)	19,341 feet
	Kenya (Kenya)	17,058 feet
Antarctica	Vinson	16,066 feet
	Tyree	16,290 feet
Asia	Everest (Tibet/Nepal)	29,028 feet
	K2 (Kashmir/Sinkiang)	28,169 feet
Australasia	Cook (New Zealand)	12,349 feet
	Kosciusko (Australia)	7,310 feet
Europe	Elbrus (Russian Caucasus)	18,510 feet
	Blanc (French Alps)	15,771 feet
North America	McKinley (Alaska)	20,320 feet
	Logan (Canada)	19,524 feet
South America	Aconcagua (Argentina)	22,834 feet
	Ojos del Salada (Argentina-Chile)	22,664 feet

Continents

Asia	17,139,445 sq mi
Africa	11,677,239 sq mi
North America	9,361,791 sq mi
South America	6,880,706 sq mi
Antarctica	5,500,000 sq mi
Europe	3,997,929 sq mi
Australia	2,967,909 sq mi

Oceans

Pacific	57,523,000 sq mi
Atlantic	32,485,000 sq mi
Indian	31,507,000 sq mi
Southern (Antarctic)	12,451,000 sq mi
Arctic	5,440,000 sq mi
Caribbean Sea	1,063,000 sq mi
Mediterranean Sea	971,000 sq mi
Gulf of Mexico	596,000 sq mi

Land and Sea Puzzles

After mapmakers had mapped the continents' coastlines, people began to wonder why some of their shapes seemed to match, like interlocking pieces of a jigsaw puzzle. South America's eastern coast and the western coast of Africa in particular looked far too similar for the match to be just a coincidence.

As the years passed, scientists discovered more puzzles. Paleontologists (geologists who specialize in studying fossils) found the remains of 16-inch-long reptiles called mesosaurs in 280-million-year-old rocks in South America and in South Africa. They knew that mesosaurs lived only in fresh water, so the reptiles couldn't have swum across the Atlantic Ocean. The paleontologists concluded that Africa and South America were joined together 280 million years ago, a time when the Atlantic Ocean didn't exist.

Other geologists studied the layers of clay that ancient **ice sheets** had left behind. These clues showed that a vast sheet of ice had covered Antarctica, India, and the southern parts of Australia, South America, and Africa about 300 million years ago. For the edges of the ice-covered areas to match up so well, the continents must have been clustered together at that time.

Evidence in the Rocks
Fossils of freshwater mesosaurs, semiaquatic lystrosaurs, and the fern glossopteris show that between 280 and 180 million years ago, South America, Africa, India, Australia, and Antarctica were joined. Signs of ancient ice sheets and bands of matching rock types in Brazil and Africa and also across East Africa, Madagascar, and India tell the same story.

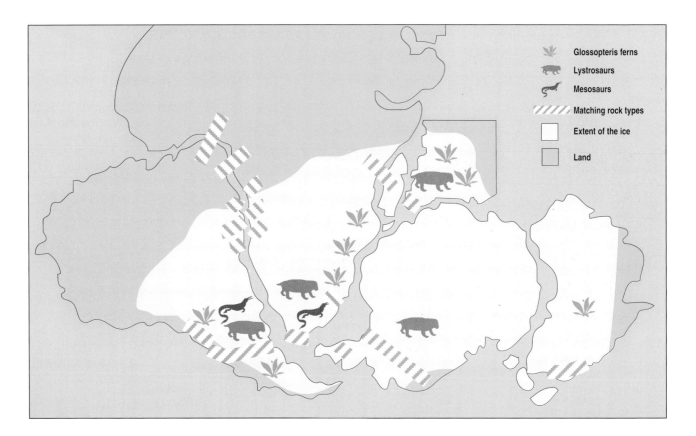

Glossopteris ferns
Lystrosaurs
Mesosaurs
Matching rock types
Extent of the ice
Land

Tiny grains of magnetic minerals in layers of old sandstone and volcanic lava provided more evidence. When the sand was soft and wet and the lava was still molten, the grains lined up with the earth's magnetic field–the force lines of the planet's own magnetism. As the rocks hardened, these tiny mineral "compass needles" were locked in place. But these days when geologists study the rocks, they find the compass needles don't always point north. The magnetic grains can't have moved inside the rocks, so the rocks themselves must have changed their position on the earth's surface.

By the early 1960s, the scientists agreed that the continents must have moved. They called the idea "continental drift" but still couldn't explain *how* it happened. Marine geologists unlocked the secret when they discovered that molten rock was rising through cracks in undersea mountain chains and moving the whole ocean floor along like a vast conveyor belt.

Above: In 1858 the Italian scientist Antonio Pelligrini suggested that South America and Africa had once been joined. People thought the idea was crazy–and dropped it!

Fossils like this dinosaur leg bone reveal how animals and plants evolved. But fossils can also provide important clues to ancient climates and to the pattern of land and sea in ages past. This is because we know that certain animals and plants lived only in deserts, or in forests, or in warm shallow seas. By plotting where these fossils are found, scientists can map the deserts, forests, and seas that existed many millions of years ago, even if modern conditions are very different.

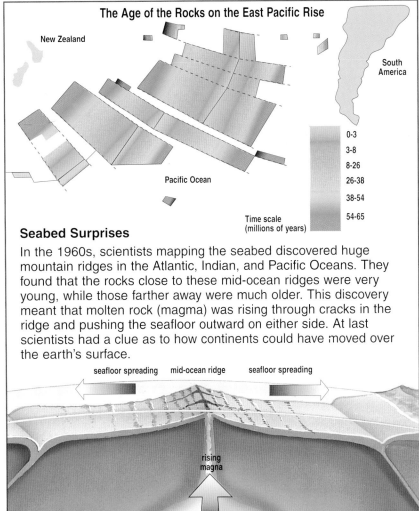

The Age of the Rocks on the East Pacific Rise

New Zealand

South America

Pacific Ocean

	0-3
	3-8
	8-26
	26-38
	38-54
	54-65

Time scale
(millions of years)

Seabed Surprises

In the 1960s, scientists mapping the seabed discovered huge mountain ridges in the Atlantic, Indian, and Pacific Oceans. They found that the rocks close to these mid-ocean ridges were very young, while those farther away were much older. This discovery meant that molten rock (magma) was rising through cracks in the ridge and pushing the seafloor outward on either side. At last scientists had a clue as to how continents could have moved over the earth's surface.

seafloor spreading   mid-ocean ridge   seafloor spreading

rising magma

Continents on the Move

When scientists discovered that the earth was creating new crust along the midocean ridges, many theories about the earth had to be revised. Scientists knew the planet was not getting any larger, so if new crust was forming in the middle of the oceans, old crust had to be disappearing from somewhere else to make room for the new crust. But where was the old crust going? Scientists found the answer in the deep trenches edging the Pacific and Indian Oceans. Beneath these trenches, the seabed conveyor dives into the earth, dragging old crust deep into the mantle layer below, where the crustal rocks are melted. Currents in the semimolten rocks of the mantle drive the system. Just like the currents in a simmering pan, the mantle currents rise in one place, spread out sideways, and then sink again somewhere else.

This discovery solved the 140-year-old puzzle of the "drifting" continents. Geologists realized that the earth's crust is made up of eight large crustal plates and several smaller ones and that the plates are being dragged across the earth's surface by the

The Earth's Fiery Regions
The margins of the earth's crustal plates are the focus of geological activity. The San Andreas fault system in California marks the line where the Pacific Plate grinds northward past the North American Plate. For years at a time, the plates stick. But the strain continues to build up, and eventually the rocks give way and skid past one another with a jolt, releasing the powerful shock waves of an earthquake.

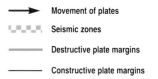

➡	Movement of plates
▪▫▪▫	Seismic zones
──	Destructive plate margins
──	Constructive plate margins

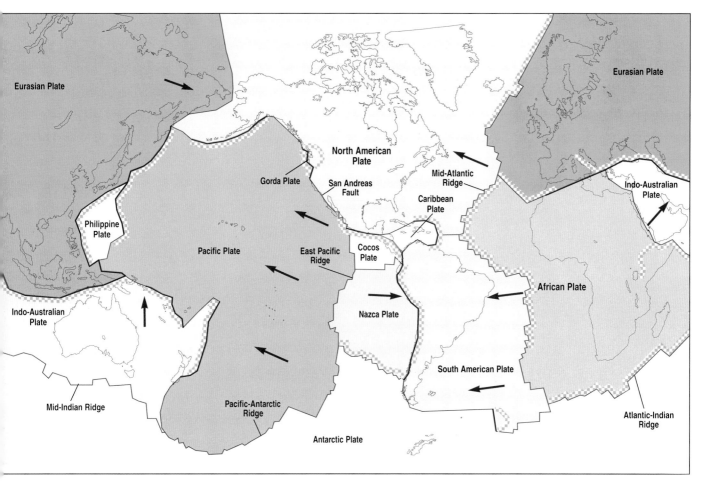

currents in the mantle below. The continents–made of lighter rocks than the seabed crust–ride along on the crustal plates like huge rafts. The fastest movement occurs at the East Pacific Rise. There the seabed grows more than six inches a year on each side of the ridge, widening the Pacific by more than a foot every year.

Plate tectonics, as this new theory was named, caused great excitement because it answered so many questions. It explained why earthquakes and volcanoes are so common around the **Pacific Rim**–an area where the edge of the Pacific Plate is being dragged down and melted. The plates grind against one another, sending out shock waves, and the melting rocks feed volcanoes on the surface far above.

The theory also explained how mountain ranges were created. They are "crumple zones" formed where one crustal plate has smashed into another. The Red Sea is a brand new ocean just starting to open up. And the long, straight lines of islands in the Pacific Ocean formed as the Pacific Plate moved slowly over the top of volcanic hot spots in the mantle.

High and Dry
Close to the summit of Mount Everest are rock layers containing fossilized sea creatures. The rocks are the remains of an ancient seafloor, crushed and bulldozed five miles into the air when India crashed into Asia.

Geology in Action
This cross section of the Pacific shows new rock rising at the ridge, pushing the seabed outward. Old crust is sinking back into the mantle at the edges, causing earthquakes and volcanoes in Japan and Southeast Asia (on the left) and in the Andes Mountains of South America (on the right).

500 million years ago   325 million years ago

Above: Five hundred million years ago, the main land areas were clustered in the Southern Hemisphere. Then two enormous fragments split off and drifted north.

The Earth's Changing Face

The earth's history stretches back more than 4.6 billion years. For the first billion or so years, nothing could have survived on the planet's surface. There was no atmosphere, the temperature was far too hot, and the thin rocky crust was covered in volcanoes and lakes of lava. But slowly the planet cooled. Steam from the volcanoes began to fall as rain and to collect on the earth's surface, first forming lakes and eventually oceans.

Microscopic one-celled plants called **algae**–the first living organisms–lived in the warm shallow seas about 3.5 billion years ago. But life evolved very slowly, so it took another two billion years for more advanced algae to develop. These algae were followed about one billion years ago by worms and other soft-bodied animals. By about 600 million years ago, the earth had an atmosphere rich in oxygen,

Between 345 and 280 million years ago, North America and Europe were still joined. Swamp forests of giant club mosses and ferns covered coastal areas. These swamps created the modern world's coal fields.

PANGAEA

Panthalassa   Panthalassa

Tethys

175 million years ago

About 275 million years ago, the three ancient continents collided, forming one huge supercontinent–Pangaea–which lasted 175 million years.

50 million years ago

Pangaea broke up about 100 million years ago. By 50 million years ago, the Atlantic had opened, and the modern world was taking shape.

50 million years from now

The continents are still moving. In 50 million years, Australia will have traveled north, and part of East Africa will have split off.

From 280 to 135 million years ago, the earth was ruled by a succession of amazing reptiles, ranging from chicken-sized sprinters to rumbling heavyweights with spiked armor and massive horned head-shields.

and evolution speeded up. Trilobites, corals, shellfish, and fishes developed in the oceans. About 420 million years ago, the first **amphibians** moved onto the land, which by then was clothed in mosses and primitive tree-sized ferns. From about 230 million years ago to 65 million years ago, reptiles–the dinosaurs and their relatives–ruled. When the reptiles faded, the mammals took over, along with a huge variety of plants, birds, fishes, and insects. Humans, the new kids on the block, only appeared a few million years ago.

Over its long history, the earth's face has continued to change. Continents have moved apart, collided, joined, and broken apart again. Climatic changes have covered vast areas of land in ice sheets, deserts, and seas. Rain, wind, rivers, and glaciers are constantly shaping and reshaping the landscape. Scientists can figure out roughly where the continents will be in another 50 million years. What they can't predict is what the landscape will look like then or what new kinds of plants and animals might have evolved.

15

World Climates

Climate is the pattern of weather you would expect at a specific place over the course of a year. The weather can change from day to day or even from hour to hour, but climate averages the variations so the annual pattern remains constant year after year. Deserts, for example, have occasional violent rainstorms, but for most of the year deserts are dry. Northwestern Europe and the northwestern United States have occasional droughts (long dry spells), but the overall climate of these areas is mild and damp.

Climate is made up of many different aspects of weather, such as temperature, rainfall, humidity (how damp the air is), and wind. The most important of these conditions are temperature and rainfall–especially the way they vary throughout the year. Places near the **equator** get the most intense sunshine, so they are warm year-round. Warm air carries much more water vapor than cold air does, so equatorial regions have a good annual supply of rain that results in warm, moist conditions throughout the year. There is very little seasonal change

Climate differs as the earth's surface curves away from the equator toward the poles. The sun's rays are more spread out, so climates are cooler. The earth's tilt also makes the seasons much more pronounced. The **temperate regions** have four distinct seasons–spring, summer, fall, and winter. When the North Pole tips toward the sun, it's summer in the Northern Hemisphere and winter in the Southern Hemisphere. Six months later, the Southern Hemisphere is enjoying lots of sunshine, while the Northern Hemisphere has the short days, cool temperatures, and damp weather of winter.

In temperate regions like Europe and the northeastern United States, the seasons are very pronounced. In fact the fall colors in New England are so spectacular that tourists come from all over the world to see them.

The sun's rays are most concentrated in the **tropics,** where the sun is almost overhead. As you travel farther from the equator, the same amount of sunlight passes through a larger volume of atmosphere and is spread over a broader area of the earth's surface, so the sun's heat lessens.

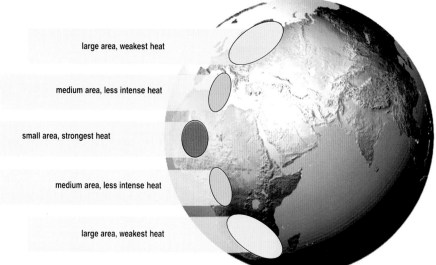

large area, weakest heat

medium area, less intense heat

small area, strongest heat

medium area, less intense heat

large area, weakest heat

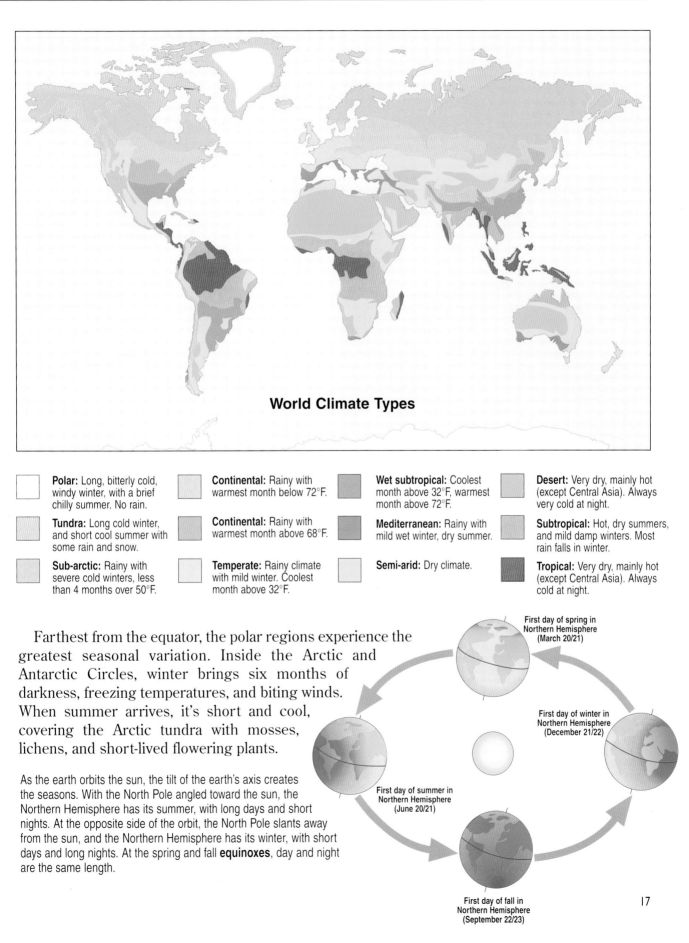

World Climate Types

Polar: Long, bitterly cold, windy winter, with a brief chilly summer. No rain.	**Continental:** Rainy with warmest month below 72°F.	**Wet subtropical:** Coolest month above 32°F, warmest month above 72°F.	**Desert:** Very dry, mainly hot (except Central Asia). Always very cold at night.	
Tundra: Long cold winter, and short cool summer with some rain and snow.	**Continental:** Rainy with warmest month above 68°F.	**Mediterranean:** Rainy with mild wet winter, dry summer.	**Subtropical:** Hot, dry summers, and mild damp winters. Most rain falls in winter.	
Sub-arctic: Rainy with severe cold winters, less than 4 months over 50°F.	**Temperate:** Rainy climate with mild winter. Coolest month above 32°F.	**Semi-arid:** Dry climate.	**Tropical:** Very dry, mainly hot (except Central Asia). Always cold at night.	

Farthest from the equator, the polar regions experience the greatest seasonal variation. Inside the Arctic and Antarctic Circles, winter brings six months of darkness, freezing temperatures, and biting winds. When summer arrives, it's short and cool, covering the Arctic tundra with mosses, lichens, and short-lived flowering plants.

As the earth orbits the sun, the tilt of the earth's axis creates the seasons. With the North Pole angled toward the sun, the Northern Hemisphere has its summer, with long days and short nights. At the opposite side of the orbit, the North Pole slants away from the sun, and the Northern Hemisphere has its winter, with short days and long nights. At the spring and fall **equinoxes**, day and night are the same length.

First day of spring in Northern Hemisphere (March 20/21)

First day of winter in Northern Hemisphere (December 21/22)

First day of summer in Northern Hemisphere (June 20/21)

First day of fall in Northern Hemisphere (September 22/23)

Desert vegetation **(top)** consists of dry grasses and thorn bushes and oddly shaped cacti that store water in their thick stems. But within days of a rain shower, millions of buried seeds sprout, produce flowers, and die quickly. Rain forest vegetation **(center)** keeps growing and flowering year-round, but the savanna **(bottom)** has contrasting seasons–parched and yellow in the dry season but covered in lush green grass in the short rainy season.

Vegetation Zones

Compare the previous climate map to the vegetation map on the page opposite. The two maps do differ in some details. But the sizes and shapes of the areas and the overall patterns they create are similar, because climate helps determine which plants will grow in a particular region. Soil type is important because it provides the nutrients (essential chemicals) that plants need to grow. The amount of sunlight is another critical element, because plants use the sun's energy to drive the chemical processes that keep them alive and healthy. But the amount of rainfall a region receives is the most significant factor. Nothing can live without water, even though some plants survive on amazingly small amounts.

Tropical rain forests are home to the richest and most varied plant life. Thousands of different species of trees, shrubs, ferns, mosses, climbers, and other plants can live in a space smaller than a football field. Year-round sunlight and water create little seasonal variation. Plants grow and flower continuously, providing food for a vast variety of animal life.

The rain forests are surrounded by **savanna**–a grassland dotted with clumps of trees. Other partly wooded or shrubby grasslands include Argentina's pampas and the chaparral of the western United States. Savannas are usually warm, with distinct wet and dry seasons. In cooler, drier, inland areas–the U.S. prairies, the steppes of Asia, and Africa's high veld–the grasslands are treeless.

Vegetation zones rarely have distinct boundaries. As conditions get drier, woodland and forest gradually give way to grassland and desert. Most deserts–like the Sahara, the Mojave, and the Great Australian–are hot, but the vast Gebi (or Gobi) Desert of central China is a bitterly cold wilderness of stony soils with scattered grasses and shrubs.

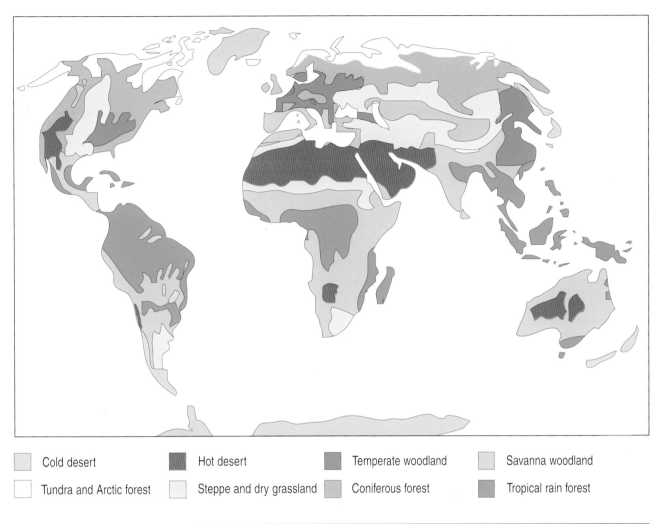

Cold desert	Hot desert	Temperate woodland	Savanna woodland
Tundra and Arctic forest	Steppe and dry grassland	Coniferous forest	Tropical rain forest

Using Vegetation Maps

The simplified map above shows only the main types of vegetation. Biologists and other specialists develop maps with dozens of categories and subdivisions. Agricultural scientists, for example, use detailed maps of vegetation, climate, and soil to advise farmers which crops will grow best on their land.

Right: Yosemite National Park is a mixed temperate woodland region with a great variety of vegetation. Deciduous trees **(foreground)** grow alongside conifers **(background)**, and the ground is covered with grasses, mosses, ferns, and wild flowers.

World Population

For several million years after humans appeared on the earth, the population remained quite small. Even 10,000 years ago–the start of the Neolithic period–there were probably only about 10 million people. But populations don't grow steadily. They grow faster and faster. By about 2000 B.C., the world's population had passed 100 million. By A.D. 1000, it had increased to about 275 million. And it was well over 500 million by A.D. 1650. By mid-1997, the number of people had soared to 5.84 billion and is still rising–at a rate of 1.5 percent per year. If the number of people continues to increase at this rate, the world's population could double by the year 2045.

Populations increase because the number of people born each year (the birth rate) is greater than the number of people who die (the death rate). People in developed countries (those with a high standard of living because they've developed their natural resources and industries) generally limit the number of children they have. They also have access to better food and health care. The result is that population growth is quite slow, and the death rate is low. By contrast, in many developing countries (those that have a low standard of living because they are just beginning to develop their natural resources and have few industries), birth rates are high. And even though their death rates are also high (compared to the United States or Europe), there are still many more births than deaths. As a result, the population of developing countries is increasing rapidly. The populations of some African countries are growing so fast that they could double in less than 25 years.

A visit to crowded Mexico City, Mexico, or Calcutta, India, might lead you to think the earth will soon be "standing room only." Of course that isn't true. Huge areas of land–Alaska, the steppes of Central Asia, and North Africa's deserts–have hardly any people at all. The problem is that people become concentrated in areas that can most easily provide them with the things they need. Coastal regions are ideal places for fishing and trading. Fertile lowlands make the best farmland. Industrial regions develop near coal fields and other mineral deposits. And as towns grow, they attract people who are looking for work.

The Way We Live
More than three-quarters of Kenya's 26 million people live in small villages **(below)**. Journeys to the nearest town are made on foot or in a local bus. An old German city **(bottom)** is typical of European urban life. Buildings are well kept, with power, water, and sewerage. The roads are lit, and the people have a range of transport options. In Hong Kong **(opposite)** the wealth and success of the commercial center contrasts strongly with the homes of the boat-dwellers who crowd the harbors.

Los An

People per square mile
2-25
25-125
125-250
more than 250
more than 10 million inhabitants

World Population Density

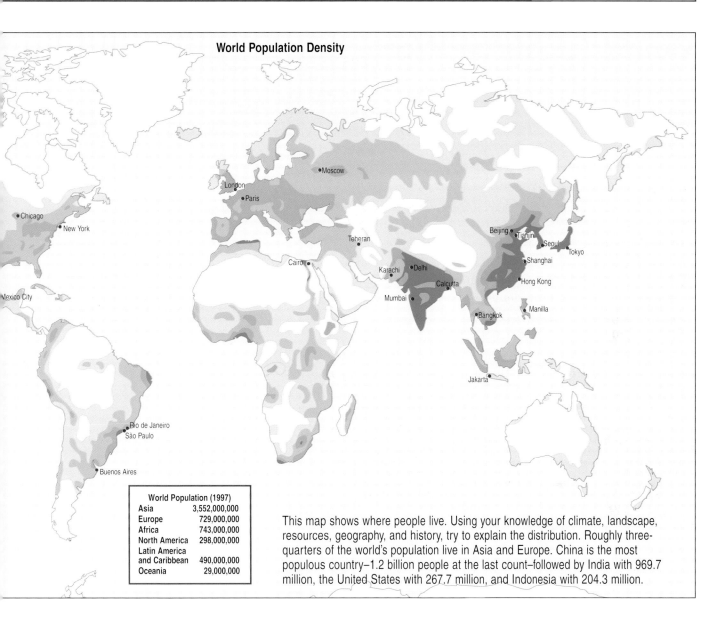

World Population (1997)	
Asia	3,552,000,000
Europe	729,000,000
Africa	743,000,000
North America	298,000,000
Latin America and Caribbean	490,000,000
Oceania	29,000,000

This map shows where people live. Using your knowledge of climate, landscape, resources, geography, and history, try to explain the distribution. Roughly three-quarters of the world's population live in Asia and Europe. China is the most populous country—1.2 billion people at the last count—followed by India with 969.7 million, the United States with 267.7 million, and Indonesia with 204.3 million.

Countries of the World

Do you know how many countries there are? That's not as simple as it sounds, because the numbers keep changing. Wars, revolutions, and even peaceful political changes require adjusting and updating the world map. Over the last few hundred years, the changes have been quite dramatic. In North America in the mid-1700s, for example, the 13 original British-ruled colonies formed a narrow strip along the Atlantic Coast from present-day Massachusetts to Georgia. Spain controlled the land to the south, while France claimed the land to the west and north. It took more than 100 years of wars, negotiations, treaties, and land purchases to create the modern-day United States.

Similar situations have occurred all over the world. Europe's national boundaries have changed countless times over the centuries, and new countries have appeared in Africa, Asia, and the Caribbean as former European colonies have gained their independence.

In 1997 there were 192 independent countries, each of which has its own territory, currency, and systems of law and government. Independent countries are responsible for their own affairs and are recognized by other independent countries as political units. Most countries consist mainly of people who share a common language, religion, or culture, although many countries contain people of diverse backgrounds.

The breakup of the Soviet Union in 1991 changed the world map yet again. Each of its 15 republics–some lying in Asia and some in eastern Europe–declared their independence. The disintegration of Yugoslavia and the Arab–Israeli conflicts in the Middle East have also required adjustments to the world map.

The Many Faces of Nationhood
The Capitol Building **(left)** in Washington, D.C., is not just the home of one branch of the U.S. government, it's a symbol of democracy to people all over the world. The return of Hong Kong to China **(right)** after 99 years under British rule was an example of peaceful political change. Rebels forced these refugees in Rwanda **(far right)** to flee with whatever they could carry.

Families of Nations

When groups of nations work together to help and support one another, they are much stronger and more successful than they would be working alone. Dozens of such groups, called international organizations, exist and they have several purposes. Some are military, some concentrate on trade and economic matters, while others focus on social and cultural affairs.

Headquartered in New York, New York, the United Nations (UN) is the world's largest international organization. Many of the countries that fought in World War II set up the UN after the war ended in 1945. They decided to establish an organization dedicated to preventing war and injustice and to improving the quality of life for people throughout the world. Fifty founding members signed the original UN charter, and since then more than 130 additional

European Union (EU)
The aim of the European Union **(above)** is to bring the economies, social systems, and political systems of the member states closer together. Other countries are applying to join the 15-member union. Each member state still has its own government, but the union's government–the Commission of the European Union–can also pass laws that apply to all the member states.

Organization for Economic Cooperation and Development (OECD)
The OECD **(top right)** is an association of 29 countries in North America, Europe, Australasia, and the Far East. Its aims are to improve the economic and social welfare of its own citizens and to provide help to the developing countries. In recent years, the OECD has also developed close contacts with non-member countries in Asia, Latin America, and the former Soviet Union.

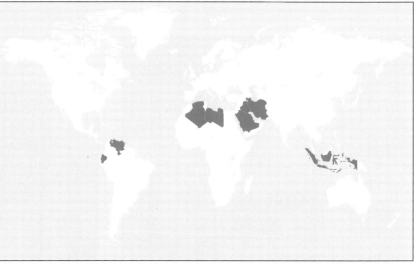

Organization of Petroleum Exporting Countries (OPEC)
OPEC **(right)** is one of the world's most important and powerful trade alliances. Its members control the supply–and the price–of roughly three-quarters of the world's oil.

United Nations (UN)

The UN was created in 1945. Its aim was to encourage cooperation between nations and to prevent future wars. Each member nation is represented at the General Assembly **(below)** which meets at the headquarters building in New York **(left)**. The UN's biggest task is helping to maintain peace in the world's trouble spots, but the organization has many other specialized agencies. UN peace-keeping forces can include soldiers from any of the UN Member States. Their task is to keep warring groups apart until political solutions to their problems can be found.

countries have joined. Every member-country is represented at the General Assembly, and each has one vote on all issues. The 15-member Security Council is the main peace-keeping agency. It has five permanent members–China, France, Russia, the United Kingdom, and the United States–and 10 other members elected to two-year terms by the General Assembly. The Economic and Social Council has 54 members elected by the General Assembly to serve for three years at a time. This large council is responsible for 16 specialized agencies that oversee health, education, agriculture, finance, and other matters. They include the World Health Organization (WHO), the Food and Agriculture Organization (FAO), and the World Bank. The UN's International Court of Justice, headquartered at the Hague in the Netherlands, handles international legal disputes.

Feeding the World

In addition to nutrients, food contains energy (measured in calories) that the body uses as fuel. To be healthy, people need the right mixture of nutrients in their diet and also the right number of calories. In theory there is enough food in the world to feed everyone. The problem is that much of it is far from those who need it.

North America and Europe grow and process far more food than they need to feed their populations. Their temperate climates, fertile soils, and modern farming methods make them very productive areas. In fact farmers in these areas produce so much food that the surplus is sometimes destroyed because it can't always be transported–without spoiling–to parts of the world where people are hungry. And even if there were enough refrigerated trucks to deliver the food, refrigerators are rare in the remote villages of Africa where many of the world's hungry people live. The result of this imbalance is that North America and Europe, with about 18 percent of the world's population between them, produce 47 percent of the world's food, while Asia and Africa, with almost 75 percent of the world's mouths to feed, produce only 43 percent of the food.

Diets vary enormously throughout the world, but each one includes a staple (one basic food) that provides most of the food energy, usually in the form of starches and sugars (also

Calories per day

More than 3,500

3,000-3,500

2,500-3,000

2,000-2,500

Less than 2,000

The shops and supermarkets in developed countries offer a wide range of healthy foods, both home grown and imported. They include fresh fruits and vegetables, meat and fish, eggs, dairy products, and a variety of canned and frozen foods.

Well Fed or Hungry?
This map shows how many calories of food energy people take in each day. Across most of Africa and large parts of southern Asia, millions of people survive on less than the 2,600 calories per day that the World Health Organization estimates is the minimum for a healthy active life.

For millions of people in the world's poorest countries, the main (or only) meal of the day consists of a handful of boiled rice, perhaps with a few vegetables. Children who grow up on this kind of diet suffer from many diseases caused by lack of vitamins, minerals, and other nutrients.

known as carbohydrates). Cereals such as wheat, rice, maize, millet, and sorghum are the world's main staple foods. In some regions, root crops like potatoes are important. Proteins are needed for building bones and muscles. We get animal protein from meat, fish, eggs, and dairy products and plant protein from cereals and vegetables, but legumes (peas and beans) are the best protein source. We also need vitamins and minerals. Although the amounts we need are small, these chemicals are essential to good health. Lack of vitamins and minerals causes many diseases, especially in countries with low or unvaried food supplies.

Health and Education

To lead active, healthy lives, we need a balanced diet, clean drinking water, proper sanitation, and public-health regulations to prevent the spread of disease. We also need access to health-care specialists when we are ill or injured. Those who live in developed countries are extremely fortunate. Americans, Canadians, and Europeans, for example, enjoy roughly 1 professional health-care worker for every 150 people, and in New Zealand the statistic is nearly 1 to 70. By contrast, in many of the world's poorest countries each health-care worker is spread between 5,000 to 6,000 people, and millions of people never see a doctor, dentist, nurse, or midwife.

The global differences in food and water quality and in health care have a dramatic effect on how long people live. In the United States, a man can expect to live about 73 years and a woman about 79. Of developed countries, though, Japan tops the list at 77 years for men and nearly 83 for women. In the poorer countries of Africa–such as Mali, Sierra Leone, and Ethiopia–the average lifespan for a man is around 45 and for a woman is about 48.

Education is another issue with great global disparity. More than 80 percent of young people in the developed countries attend secondary school, but in parts of South America and in most of Africa, India, and Southeast Asia, less than 40 percent attend school. In some of the poorest countries, less than one-fourth of the population can read and write. International groups like the UN and voluntary organizations like the U.S. Peace Corps are helping these countries improve their education, health, and welfare systems.

Caring and Protecting
Families in developed countries have easy access to dentists and doctors. Children receive regular medical checkups and vaccinations to protect them against a wide range of illnesses.

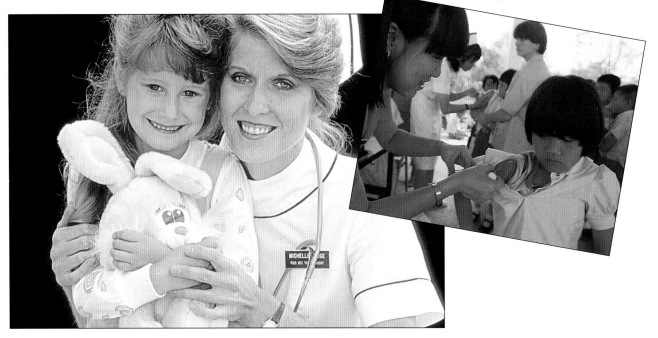

The number of babies and infants who die before their first birthday is a reminder of how inadequate health care is in many of the world's poorest countries.

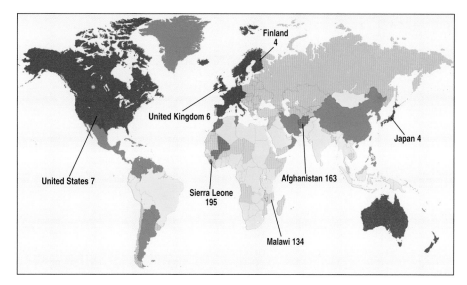

■ More than 150 deaths per 1,000 births
▢ 100-150 deaths per 1,000 births
▢ 50-100 deaths per 1,000 births
▤ 20-50 deaths per 1,000 births
▤ 10-20 deaths per 1,000 births
■ Less than 10 deaths per 1,000 births

The percentage of the population who are illiterate (unable to read or write) indicates the countries that have less money to spend on education. Canada and Sweden spend about US$1000 a year per person on education. The United States and Switzerland spend around US$800. In Chad, Nepal, Bangladesh, and Ethiopia, spending is less than US$5 per person.

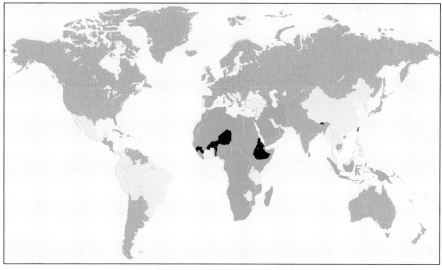

■ More than 75% of population unable to read or write
▤ 50-75% of population unable to read or write
▤ 25-50% of population unable to read or write
▢ 10-15% of population unable to read or write
▤ Less than 10% of population unable to read or write

The ratio of people to health-care workers, country by country, shows at a glance which countries have the money and training facilities to provide good health services.

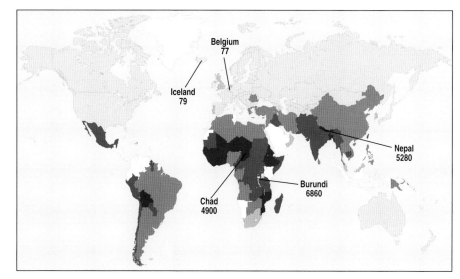

■ 3000-6000 people per health worker
■ 1000-3000 people per health worker
▤ 370-1000 people per health worker
▤ 150-370 people per health worker
▢ Less than 150 people per health worker
▢ No data

Imbalanced Resources

Lending a Hand
On July 13, 1985, two simultaneous 16-hour rock concerts were played at the JFK Stadium in Philadelphia, Pennsylvania, and at Wembley Stadium in London, England. Hundreds of rock stars and technicians gave their time free. People donated millions of dollars to help the hungry in the drought-striken countries of Africa.

One way to look at the world so we can better understand it is to divide it between developed (rich) countries that have many resources and less-developed (poor) countries that have very few. In rich countries, most people live in homes with clean water, proper sanitation, and some kind of heating. They generally have access to nutritious food and decent health care. Most families own cars, TVs, telephones, and various labor-saving devices. That doesn't mean that everyone in a rich country is personally wealthy. Even rich countries like the United States, Australia, Japan, and Germany have impoverished areas. The difference between these areas and poor countries is that developed nations almost always have a support system. People who find themselves in serious trouble can usually take advantage of a state welfare system.

Long-term Aid
Villagers at Chunga in Zimbabwe watch as fresh water is drawn from a new well dug by one of the international aid agencies. This kind of help is vital in poor countries. A guaranteed supply of clean water will protect the health of the villagers and enable them to grow crops even in times of low rainfall.

Gross domestic product (GDP) is one way of measuring how rich a country is. GDP is the total value of all goods and services produced in a country in a year. It includes the money people spend on food, clothes, cars, TVs, insurance, and holidays; the money businesses spend on new factories and machines; the money the government spends on roads, schools, hospitals, and defense; and the country's profits from the goods it sells to other countries. The total value is divided by the population to create a per capita (per person) figure, a convenient way of comparing one country with another.

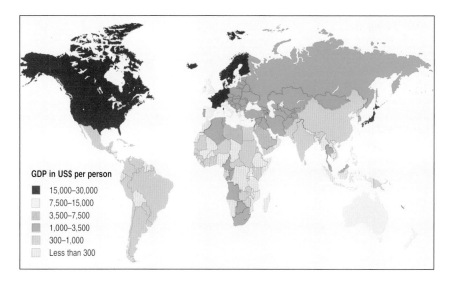

GDP in US$ per person

- 15,000–30,000
- 7,500–15,000
- 3,500–7,500
- 1,000–3,500
- 300–1,000
- Less than 300

The poorest countries of the world aren't as fortunate. Millions of people face hardship without a state welfare system to help them. Poverty and malnutrition (shortage of vitamins, minerals, and other nutrients) are especially serious in the drought-ridden countries of Equatorial Africa–from Mali and Burkina Faso to Ethiopia and Somalia. When the rains fail in these already dry countries, entire crops are lost. Hundreds of thousands of people already weak from hunger and malnutrition face famine and widespread diseases. Their only chance for survival is the food, medicines, blankets, and fresh water sent by aid organizations such as the United Nations Children's Fund (UNICEF), the Red Cross, the Red Crescent, Save the Children, CARE, and OXFAM.

The Haves and the Have-nots
The graph below indicates how many luxuries people in developed countries enjoy. By showing the number of TVs, cars, and phones are owned per 10,000 people.

Cars   T.V.   Telephones

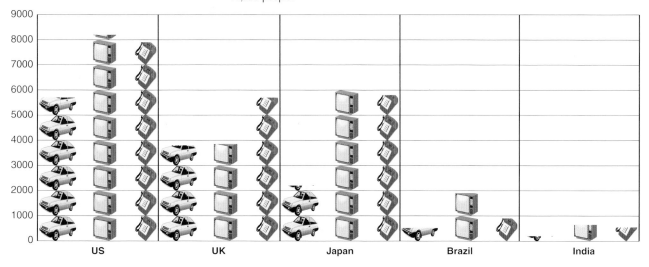

US   UK   Japan   Brazil   India

Land Use and Farming

How much of the land we use–and what we use it for–depends on several factors. Deserts are too hot and dry to be farmed without costly irrigation, and the polar areas are too cold. However, these regions are still useful. They contain some of the world's most important oil and gas fields. Mountains can also be productive, supporting tourism, quarrying, mining, and terraced farming.

Temperate and tropical regions with adequate rainfall devote a large proportion of the land to agriculture. In fact almost one-third of the earth's total land area is farmed. Farmers use about one-third of their land for growing crops and the remaining two-thirds for pasturing livestock. Climate determines which crops grow best and where. Bananas, cacao beans, and pineapples, for example, need tropical conditions, while potatoes, wheat,

Above: Asian farmers make use of steep slopes by building terraces for rice and other crops. Water is channelled into the upper terraces and allowed to trickle downward, gently watering the crops below without washing away the precious soil. **Below:** In Europe and the United States, fertile land is plentiful on flat or gently rolling land.

Right: Pie diagrams are useful tools for comparing land use in different regions. You can see at a glance how much of South America is forest, and how intensively Europe is farmed.

Forest
Crop lands
Pasture and rough grazing
Non-productive land
Orchards and plantations

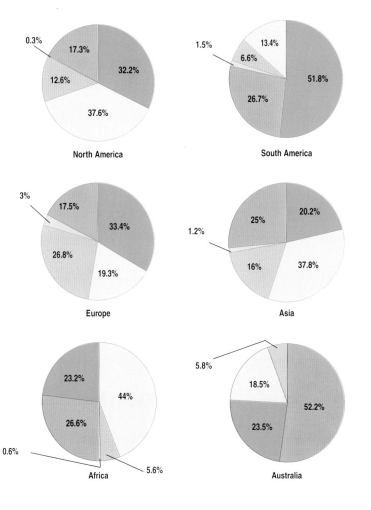

North America

South America

Europe

Asia

Africa

Australia

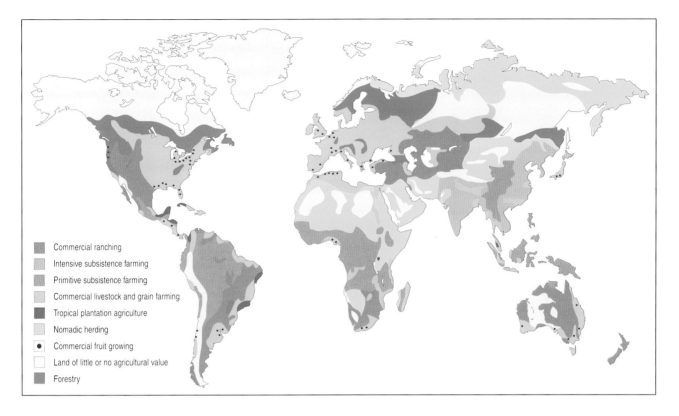

Commercial ranching
Intensive subsistence farming
Primitive subsistence farming
Commercial livestock and grain farming
Tropical plantation agriculture
Nomadic herding
Commercial fruit growing
Land of little or no agricultural value
Forestry

This map can provide only a generalized picture of agricultural land use around the world. Pick an area you don't know very well, and use your school and public libraries to find out more about what people grow there, what animals they raise, and the farming methods they use. Commercial farmers produce crops and animals to sell, often to big companies that process the food and pack it for stores and for export. Subsistence farmers are small-scale farmers who just produce enough to feed their own families.

and apples thrive in cooler climates. Some crops, such as rice and potatoes, need a lot of water. Others, like sorghum and barley, prefer drier climates.

Forests cover roughly another third of the earth's land area. In the past, forests blanketed much more of the world, but over the centuries we've cut them down to create farmland. In western Europe and the United States, less than 5 percent of the original forests remain, although Canada and northern Asia still have large expanses of old evergreen forests.

Human actions have also greatly reduced vegetation in tropical rain forests where soils are typically not suited for farming. Loggers have cut much of the rain forests in South America, West Africa, and Indonesia, and ranchers have cleared large tracts to raise livestock. Small-scale farmers also do some clearing, often using the slash-and-burn method. After clearing vegetation, they burn the stumps and plant crops. Often the crops don't do well in the weak tropical soil. After harvests fail, the farmers repeat the process on another plot. Without trees to hold down the soil, it gets washed into the rivers by heavy rains.

Towns, cities, and industrial land uses such as mines and quarries cover a surprisingly small amount of land. In the United States, these forms of land use take up less than 3 percent of the land. The percentage is even lower worldwide.

Where Did That Come From?

People have been trading for thousands of years. One system, called bartering, involves no money. You locate someone who has a surplus of the item you want, and you negotiate a trade, or swap, in exchange for some of your own surplus goods. The more common method is to sell your spare goods for money, which you can then use to buy the things you need. Using money gives you more options because you can sell to one person but buy from someone else.

Types of trade vary from country to country. The United States, for example, has fertile land, good supplies of water, and large reserves of coal, oil, and minerals. It's well supplied with food, energy, and basic raw materials. As a result, almost three-fourths of U.S. imports (goods that are brought into the country) and exports (goods sold to other countries) are manufactured items such as cars, cameras, computers, and clothes. The United States trades mostly with other manufacturing countries, including Canada, Japan, and European nations.

Europe's total trade surpasses that of the United States but is made up of different items. Europe is small, crowded, and very

Producing for Export

Bananas grow well in hot, damp climates. They are rich in energy (sugar), minerals, and vitamins and are popular all over the world. The fruits are a major cash crop in Brazil, Uganda, India, Malaysia, the Philippines, Colombia, and Ecuador. Big international companies develop and control production and reap high profits. Only a small part of the profit goes to the countries in which the fruit is grown.

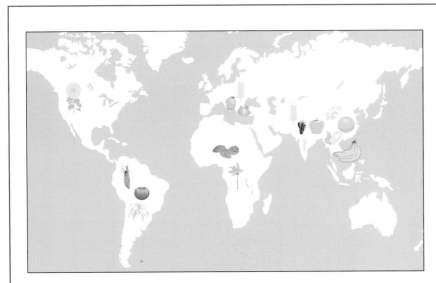

North America: sunflowers

Latin America: tomatoes, maize, potatoes, cotton, tobacco, rubber

Africa: palm oil, sorghum, millet, coffee

China-Japan: soybeans, oranges, rice, tea

Europe-North Asia: oats, rye

Mediterranean: sugar beets, cabbages, rapeseed, olives

West-Central Asia: wheat, barley, grapes, apples, linseed, flax

India: jute, rice

Southeast Asia: bananas, coconuts, sugarcane, yams

Where Did Tomatoes Come From?

Next time you are in a supermarket, look at the huge variety of different foods. You might be surprised how many of them originated in countries far away even if these days many of them are grown all over the world.

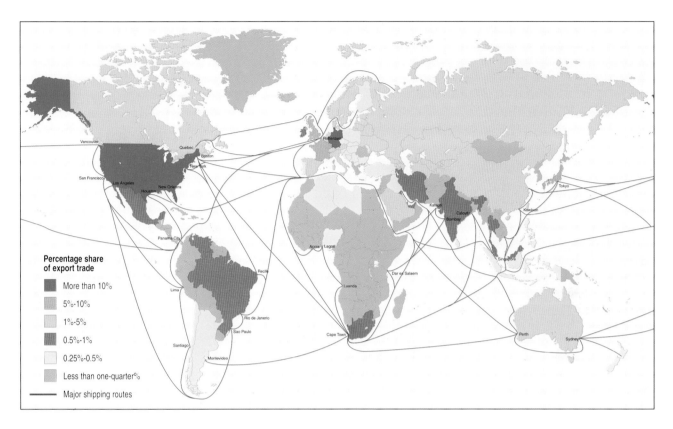

Percentage share of export trade

- More than 10%
- 5%-10%
- 1%-5%
- 0.5%-1%
- 0.25%-0.5%
- Less than one-quarter%
- Major shipping routes

industrialized. The continent needs more fuel and raw materials than it can produce. Europe imports lots of fuel, timber, metals, chemicals, cotton, wool, and other raw materials. These goods come from all over the world. To pay for them, Europeans sell manufactured goods, food, and financial services (such as banking). Most developing countries are short of food and farm supplies (fertilizers, seed, and tractors). To earn the money to buy these supplies, they often have to sell their timber and minerals or use their best agricultural land for growing **cash crops**–the ones that other countries most want to buy.

A handful of developed countries dominate world trade. The United States, Germany, Japan, France, the United Kingdom, Italy, and Canada account for more than half of the world's total exported goods.

Right: Traders in the New York Stock Exchange buy and sell shares in companies all over the world. Other financial traders deal in foreign currencies (money), insurance, and banking services. These activities all make money, even though no goods are produced, so they are included in a nation's GDP as "invisible earnings."

Minerals under the Surface

Industries tend to develop near the raw materials they use. Here's an example. Rocks that lie beneath the Great Lakes region of the Midwest are rich in iron ore, the main ingredient in steel. It's no surprise, then, that the U.S. auto industry became centered in Detroit, Michigan, a city on Lake Erie. Likewise, Cleveland, Ohio, and Pittsburgh, Pennsylvania (also both on Lake Erie), and Chicago, Illinois, and Milwaukee, Wisconsin (both on Lake Michigan), became the country's leading steel and heavy machinery producers. Miners extract limestone, another essential ingredient in steel, in Ohio. Coal–used to fuel the smelters (which melt the ore to extract the metal)–comes from Virginia, Pennsylvania, and Ohio.

Mineral concentrations can be found in many parts of the world. One large iron ore field stretches across the Kiruna region of Sweden. Montana, Utah, Arizona, and New Mexico mine nearly 90 percent of U.S. copper. The most important source of nickel is the Sudbury region of Ontario, Canada. And the main producers of bauxite, the ore from which aluminum is made, are Guyana, Jamaica, and Suriname. But not all mineral deposits are conveniently placed. Large deposits of some ores are found far from the industrial centers that need them. Congo (formerly Zaire) and Zambia, for example, have large deposits of copper that are shipped out for processing in Japan, Europe, and the United States.

Most ores formed millions of years ago by a geological process deep inside the earth's rocky crust. The metals dissolved in the hot, salty, acidic waters seeping through the rocks and, as the crust cooled, they became concentrated in certain areas. Other concentrations, called placer deposits, formed more recently. Small particles of heavy minerals–such as tin, gold, titanium, and diamonds–wash into the sea, as rain and rivers wear down the land. These minerals are heavier than the silt and sand that travels with them, so the particles drop quickly to the seabed and become concentrated there.

When mineral ores lie close to the earth's surface, they can be extracted by the open pit method **(left)** using gigantic diggers and dump trucks. Deep deposits, like the coal seam **(right),** require deep mine shafts to be sunk, while placer deposits of tin off the Malaysian coast **(far right)** are worked using huge floating dredgers.

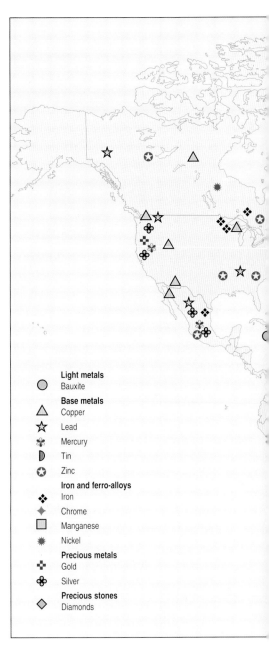

Light metals
○ Bauxite

Base metals
△ Copper
☆ Lead
✳ Mercury
◗ Tin
◎ Zinc

Iron and ferro-alloys
❖ Iron
✦ Chrome
□ Manganese
✳ Nickel

Precious metals
✤ Gold
⚛ Silver

Precious stones
◇ Diamonds

This map shows the main production areas of the most important metals. Use your library to find out what other minerals and raw materials are mined and what they are used for. Don't forget the nonmetallic minerals such as sulfur, salt, and potash and the sand, cement, and building stones used in the construction industry.

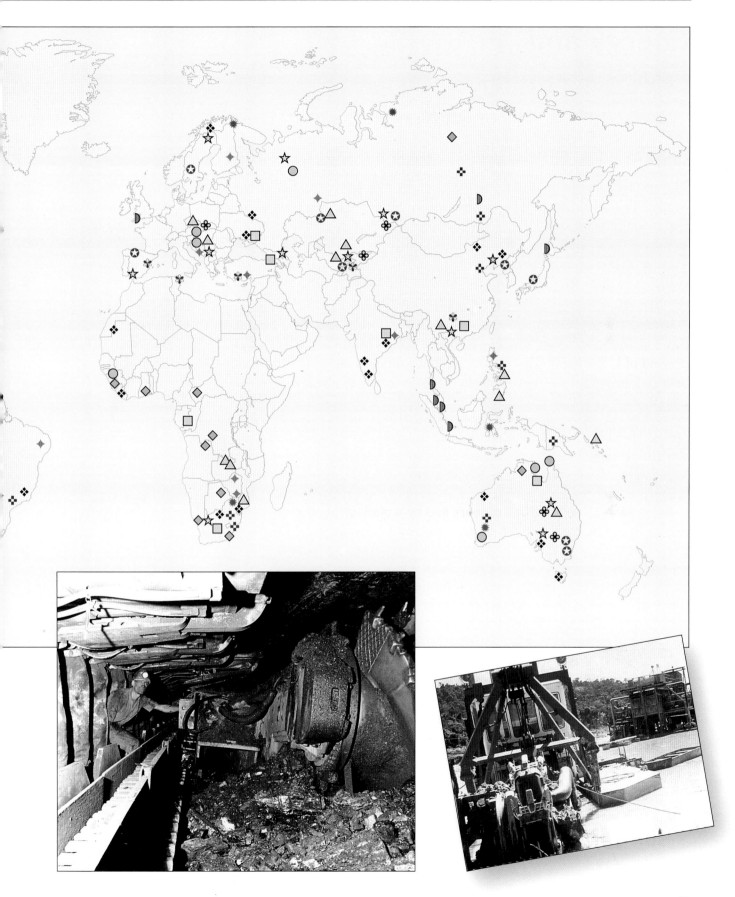

Energy and Power Supplies

Energy is one of the world's most important commodities. We can't see it, taste it, smell it, or feel it, but we use it every day. We heat and cool our homes with it. We use it to cook our food and to store food so it doesn't spoil. Energy propels our cars, trains, and aircraft and powers the industries that provide us with jobs and goods. The agricultural sector also uses a huge amount of energy–for fueling tractors, heating animal sheds, and making fertilizers, pesticides, and animal feeds.

Most of the world's energy supply comes from burning wood, coal, oil, or gas. Amazingly, more than 2 billion people depend entirely on wood for cooking and heating. Spread across the developing countries of South America, Africa, and Asia, these people face a problem. Many forests are gone, and fuel is becoming

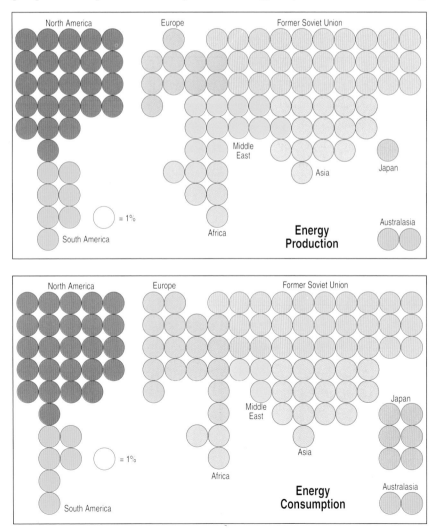

Left: When countries are drawn in proportion to the amount of energy they produce and the amount they use, we see some interesting contrasts. Japan produces only 1 percent of the world's energy but uses 5.5 percent, so that country is a major importer of energy. The Middle East has huge oil and gas reserves but relatively little industry, so the region exports nearly four times as much energy as it uses.

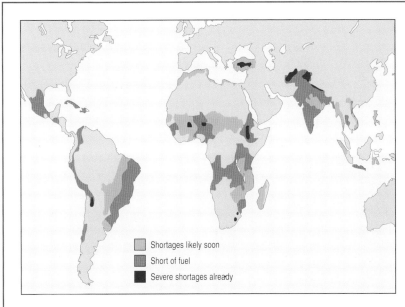

Shortages likely soon

Short of fuel

Severe shortages already

Fuelwood is so scarce in some African countries that 300 days of the year someone in the family has to spend the whole day collecting enough wood to heat the home and cook a meal.

The UN estimates that within a decade 2.4 billion people—nearly half the world's population—will not have enough fuel for heating and cooking without cutting down trees faster than new trees can grow.

more and more scarce. In parts of Niger, Mali, and Sudan, people spend many hours each day searching for enough firewood to cook a single meal.

By contrast, most people in the developed world have light and heat at the flick of a switch and easy access to transportation. About 40 percent of the energy we use is electricity—most of it made in a power station by burning coal, oil, or gas. Other ways of producing electricity come through harnessing the power of nuclear energy, the sun, wind, and water. We get the remaining 60 percent of our energy from burning gasoline and kerosene in cars and airplanes, fuel oils in ships and furnaces, coal in open fires, and gas in domestic heating and cooking appliances.

Harnessing the Elements
Solar panels (**right**) contain miles of fine tubing full of water or special oil that is heated by the sun. The hot liquid is then used to produce steam to drive the turbines of an electricity generator. Other solar panels, often used on homes or to power electrical devices like calculators, contain photovoltaic cells that convert the sun's energy directly into electricity.

Natural Disasters

In 1992 Hurricane Andrew swept across the Bahamas, southern Florida, and Louisiana, leaving 14 people dead and causing damage estimated at US$20 billion. The following year, record spring and summer rains created disastrous flooding along the Mississippi River and its tributaries. The floods left 50 people dead and 70,000 homeless across nine states. In 1994 an earthquake centered on Northridge, California, killed 55 people when buildings and elevated highways collapsed into piles of rubble.

Events like these are tragic for the people involved, but they pale in comparison to other natural disasters that have hit less developed parts of the world. A huge 1976 earthquake in northern China may have caused the deaths of 700,000 people. An earthquake in northern Iran in 1990 killed an estimated 40,000 people. And in 1991, 145 mile-per-hour hurricane winds drove 20-foot waves inland across Bangladesh, flooding hundreds of square miles of farmland. More than 125,000 people were killed, and millions were left homeless.

Some of the worst natural disasters develop slowly and last for years. Droughts have caused great misery across the Sahel region of sub-Saharan Africa–a band of parched land running from Mali to Somalia. A shift in the westerly wind pattern pushed away the seasonal rains from 1968 to 1974 and again in the mid-1980s. Crops withered, hundreds of thousands of people starved, and half the region's livestock died. International appeals paid for thousands of tons of emergency food, tents, and medical supplies, but for many the help came too late. Aid agencies continue to try to improve water supplies and farming systems across these regions to make them less vulnerable to droughts.

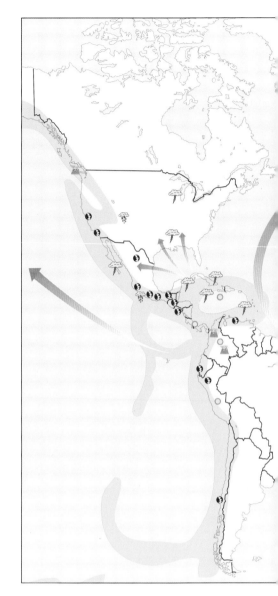

Satellite pictures reveal the true impact of natural disasters. The photographs **(left)** are of Marysville, California, before and after the floods of March 1997. In 1991 Mount Pinatubo in the Philippines **(right)** blew its top. The giant ash cloud rose 22 miles into the sky, and more than 60,000 people were evacuated. Forest fires **(far right)** happen every year in the United States, Europe, and Australia, doing millions of dollars worth of damage.

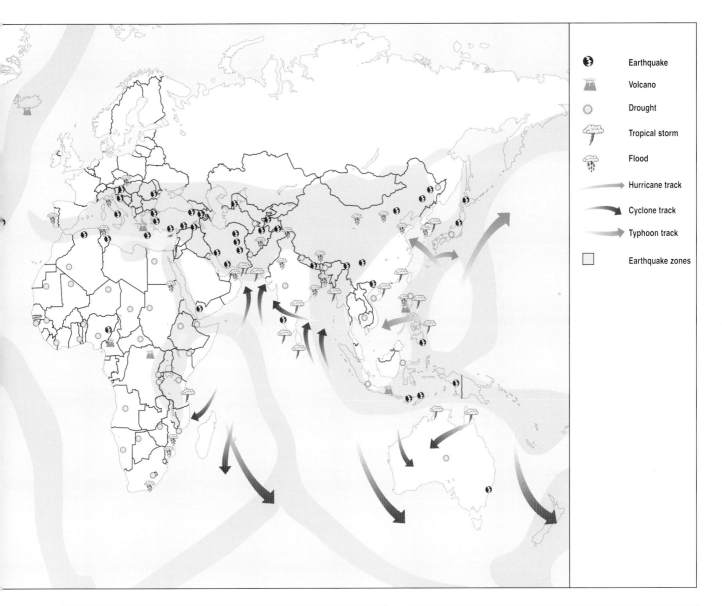

Earthquake

Volcano

Drought

Tropical storm

Flood

Hurricane track

Cyclone track

Typhoon track

Earthquake zones

Upsetting the Balance

When only a few million people inhabited the earth, smoke from their fires and waste from their villages caused very little damage. The level of damage began to change about 200 years ago, at the start of the industrial age. By then the human population had grown to well over a billion. Factory smokestacks and trains belched smoke, and industries dumped polluted water into rivers. As the industrial world grew, so did waste products–and they upset nature's delicate balance.

Some air pollution, like smoke or dust, is easy to see. But other types such as car exhaust are invisible. Traffic police, cyclists, and pedestrians in Tokyo, Japan, wear masks to protect them from car fumes. People in Los Angeles, California, and Athens, Greece, suffer from a nasty form of air pollution called photochemical smog. Caused when the sun heats car-exhaust gases, this pollutant hurts people's eyes, throats, and lungs and can also damage crops. Cars, heating systems, and factories that emit invisible gases also damage the atmosphere, which protects us from the full force of the sun's blazing rays.

Most countries have laws to protect their rivers and lakes from pollution. Many inland waterways, however, receive farm chemicals that rain washes off the land and industrial chemicals that are dumped illegally. After a chemical enters the underground water system, it can spread over vast distances.

Many countries have also signed international agreements to reduce pollution in the air and atmosphere. To decrease air pollution requires fitting factory chimneys with filters and other special equipment–an expensive process that will only succeed if developed countries help the developing ones pay the bill.

The Hole in the Ozone Layer

Between 12 and 25 miles above the earth lies a thin layer of ozone gas. The gas is actually poisonous for humans to breathe, but high in the atmosphere it forms a protective shield that blocks most of the sun's ultraviolet rays. Unfiltered, these rays cause skin cancer and other diseases and hurt many crops. Chemicals called chlorofluorocarbons (CFCs)–which are in refrigerators, spray cans, and fast-food containers–leak into the atmosphere and destroy ozone gas molecules. Manufacturers are phasing out CFCs by developing safe alternatives, but no one is sure if the phaseout is happening quickly enough.

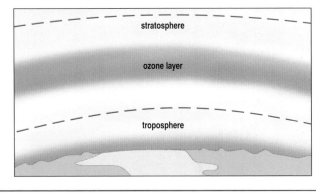

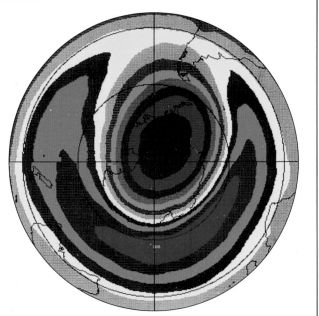

NASA scientists created this map of the ozone layer from measurements made by satellites. The dark oval region over Antarctica is the "hole." The scientists calculate that this region of the atmosphere has lost 30-40 percent of its ozone in the last 30 years.

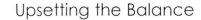

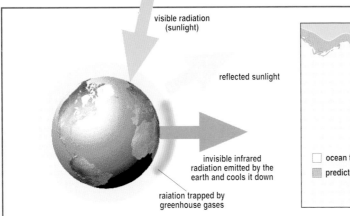

visible radiation (sunlight)

reflected sunlight

invisible infrared radiation emitted by the earth and cools it down

raiation trapped by greenhouse gases

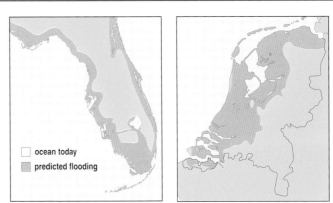

ocean today

predicted flooding

The Invisible Blanket: We already know that global temperatures are rising. Six of the seven warmest years this century occurred between 1981 and 1990.

The Greenhouse Effect

The sun's rays pass through the atmosphere and warm up the earth's surface. The earth then radiates some of this energy back into space as heat. But some gases–such as carbon dioxide, methane, and water vapor–trap this type of radiation. They act like the glass in a greenhouse–letting heat in but not letting it out again. In the last 150 years, car exhausts, factory

Flood Alert: The maps above show how much low-lying land in Florida and the Netherlands could disappear underwater if sea level rose by 10 feet.

chimneys, burning forests, and other human activities have increased the amount of heat-trapping gases in our atmosphere. Rising global temperatures already suggest that the earth is getting warmer. If the temperature continues to increase, it could alter the climate zones, making some regions too dry for agriculture. If the polar ice caps were to melt, vast areas of low-lying coastal land could be permanently flooded.

Sunsets like this are pretty to look at, but much of the spectacular color is due to pollution in the earth's atmosphere.

Habitats and Wildlife in Danger

In many parts of the world, people are damaging and even destroying natural habitats such as forests, lakes, grasslands, and marshes. Some of the damage is accidental. Some is not. Either way, the damage is nearly always permanent. Government agencies and member-supported environmental organizations work to reduce the damage. They encourage people and businesses to use the earth's resources wisely so that habitats and wildlife will be protected.

Some experts believe nearly half the world's rain forests have been cut down and that the rest will disappear in the next 30 to 50 years. When we destroy a forest, we lose more than just the trees. Other plants also die, as do the animals that depend on them for survival. The vast tropical forests also play an important part in keeping the earth's atmosphere healthy by absorbing carbon dioxide, releasing oxygen, and helping to recycle water and nutrients.

The wooded grasslands that stretch across Africa from Mali to Ethiopia are another threatened habitat. Areas that used to be thickly wooded have few trees left, and once-healthy grasslands are quickly turning into desert. Part of the problem is a succession of droughts. But some of the damage results from overgrazing livestock on the remaining vegetation.

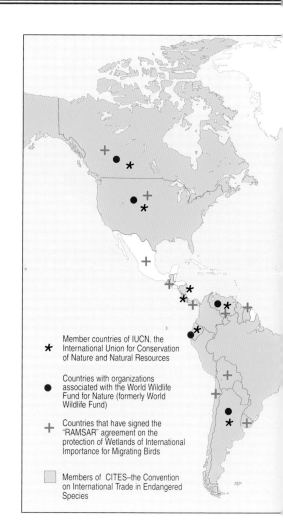

* Member countries of IUCN, the International Union for Conservation of Nature and Natural Resources

● Countries with organizations associated with the World Wildlife Fund for Nature (formerly World Wildlife Fund)

+ Countries that have signed the "RAMSAR" agreement on the protection of Wetlands of International Importance for Migrating Birds

▨ Members of CITES–the Convention on International Trade in Endangered Species

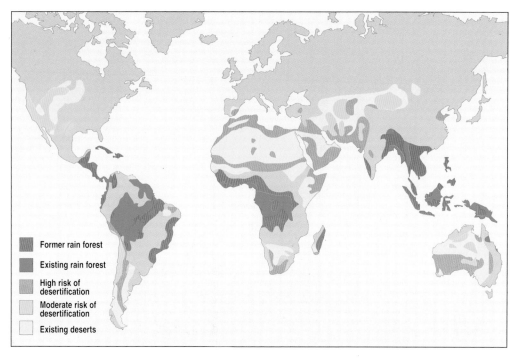

▨ Former rain forest

▨ Existing rain forest

▨ High risk of desertification

▨ Moderate risk of desertification

▨ Existing deserts

Left: People are the main cause of environmental damage. Forests are cut down for timber and to make way for farms, and deserts grow bigger as sparse vegetation is overgrazed.

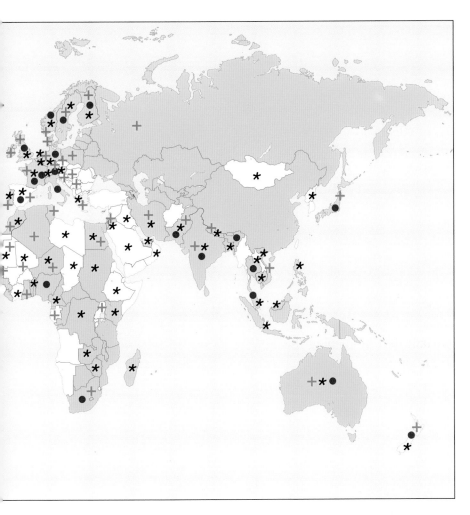

Campaigning for Change
Everyone can have a role in educating others about the importance of environmental issues, from selling rare animals **(above)** to buying souvenirs or jewelry made from the skins, feathers, and shells of endangered species.

In the developed world, industry causes the most noticeable damage. Acid rain–precipitation that contains chemicals that form acids when they combine with moisture in the air–has devastated large areas of forest in North America, Scandinavia, and central Europe. Water pollution has damaged many European and North American rivers and lakes.

Human activities, including hunting and collecting, have wiped out or brought to the brink of extinction many at-risk animals and plants. In the past, hunters and collectors didn't realize the damage they could do. These days international treaties have banned or limited hunting and collecting, showing that human actions can also bring positive change.

Conservation in Action
The map above shows countries belonging to four of the main conservation organizations that, along with UN agencies, are trying to protect rare animal and plant species and endangered habitats. But individuals can be active, too, by joining local and regional branches of environmental organizations, such as the National Wildlife Federation, the Center for Marine Conservation, the Nature Conservancy, and others. Local groups can also have an impact by organizing crews to clean up riverbanks and seashores, by raising money for conservation activities, and by collecting aluminum cans for recycling, as in this youth project.

Glossary

algae: Plants that live in water or in damp places. The most common algae are seaweeds and the green slime that forms in still ponds.

amphibian: An animal that starts its life in water, breathing through gills and then changes into an air-breathing adult with lungs. Common examples are frogs and salamanders.

cash crop: Any crop that is grown mainly for export to other countries to earn money rather than for consumption in the country in which it is grown.

continent: The name given to a large area of land. The earth's seven continents–in order of size–are Asia, Africa, North America, South America, Antarctica, Europe, and Australia.

crust: The thin, rocky outer layer of the earth.

equator: An imaginary line drawn round the globe halfway between the North and South Poles.

equinox: The date that marks the beginning of spring or fall.

ice sheet: A vast area of thick ice that covers parts of Antarctica and the Arctic but once stretched across much of the earth in ages past.

Pacific Rim: The name given to the region around the edges of the Pacific Ocean.

plate tectonics: The theory that explained continental drift, mountain building, and many other features of the earth.

resource: A material–such as water, minerals, soil, timber, food, and sources of energy–that is useful to humans.

savanna: A type of grassland with scattered clumps of trees.

temperate region: A mid-latitude area that lies between the cold polar regions and the very hot regions near the equator.

topography: The shape of the land–its mountains, valleys, plains, and ocean basins.

tropical rain forest: A dense, luxuriant type of forest that grows in the warm, wet conditions near the equator.

tropics: The broad belt centered on the equator and extending north to the Tropic of Cancer and south to the Tropic of Capricorn.

tundra: The zone between the ice and snow of the Arctic and the beginning of the northern forest zone. The tundra typically has low vegetation of mosses and lichens, with a few small, stunted trees.